MICHAEL JORDAN

A UNIQUE INSIGHT INTO THE CAREER AND MINDSET OF MICHAEL JORDAN

WHAT IT TAKES TO BE LIKE MIKE

An Unauthorized Biography
By Steve James

"The game of basketball has been everything to me. My place of refuge, place I've always gone where I needed comfort and peace. It's been the site of intense pain and the most intense feelings of joy and satisfaction. It's a relationship that has evolved over time, given me the greatest respect and love for the game."

- Michael Jordan

TABLE OF CONTENTS

INTRODUCTION

On November 1, 1994, Jerry Reinsdorf – the chairman of the Chicago Bulls, Larry King, and Michael Jordan gathered in front of the United Center before a national television audience to retire Jordan's jersey, but there was another surprise for all the viewers that tuned in to watch the ceremony: the **Michael Jordan Statue**. This 2,000-pound, 12-foot tribute, to what many consider *the greatest basketball player to ever lace up his sneakers*, is cast in bronze and depicts Jordan suspended in air over several opponents. The only point of contact between the athlete and the granite base is through Jordan's knee. Nearly a decade later, the statue boasts thousands upon thousands of US and international visitors and is still a must-see venue when tourists arrive in The Windy City.

So **what is it about Jordan that has captured the hearts and minds of the masses**, many of whom have never even picked up a basketball?

For some, it could be those gravity-defying dunks, while, for others, it's the number of points he scored per game, or even all of the titles he won. Perhaps, it could be the fact he was such a tremendous defender, while simultaneously being so offensively talented, which, to this day, is a rarity in the game of basketball. *Could it possibly be the man? His devotion to his craft? His determination to be the best, to win, and to thrive?*

It could be all of the above or none of the options offered, but one thing is for sure; Michael Jordan is a complex, talented, motivated individual who, like us all, possesses an innately human side that both contributed to and contrasted the level of excellence he achieved on the court. His amazing determination to succeed in all aspects of his life, not just basketball, seem to have contributed to the making of **one of the all-time greatest basketball players in the world**. Through this outline of Michael Jordan's talents, legacy, awards, quirks, personality, and entire history, one will find much more than just a simple biography of a legend. This brief summary of Michael Jordan's life and actions hopes to prove to every reader that Michael Jordan is indeed a legend whose actions are applicable and replicable in the daily lives

1

of every person who reads this. While not everyone has the physical abilities or the sheer luck necessary to become a basketball superstar, **everyone can learn something from being a little bit more "Like Mike"**!

CHAPTER 1

HOW IT ALL STARTED

Michael Jeffrey Jordan arrived in this world on February 17, 1963. He was James's and Deloris's third son and fourth child, as he also had an older sister. Shortly after Jordan learned how to walk, his parents decided to move their young family from Brooklyn, New York, to Wilmington, North Carolina, and the family remained there for the entirety of Jordan's childhood. His father worked as a mechanic at General Electric, and his mother worked as a bank teller in order to support the family. Jordan's family would soon welcome a final child to the family, Jordan's little sister Roslyn, after their move to Wilmington.

His early education certainly was no different than any other boy or girl his age, but the youngster did not appear to possess the desire to seriously 'hit the books' as Jordan was only an average student at best despite the attempts of his parents to alter his course. When he entered *Trask Middle School*, however, Jordan's fervor for athletics began to shine through, and he was awarded certificates of excellence for his participation in basketball and football, while also playing baseball as well. As a pitcher in the *Wilmington Little League*, Jordan threw several no-hitters and almost took his team to the World Series in Williamsport, PA. While in high school, he pitched 45 consecutive shut-out innings. His father James, whom he was very close to throughout his entire life, was enamored with baseball, but Jordan, **contrary to his father's initial wants, would decide basketball was the sport he had the most passion for.** This could be due to the influence of his older brother Larry, as Jordan thought the sun rose and set on his brother, and Larry was a basketball addict.

Sibling Rivalry:
Michael's First Motivation

Jordan's sibling rivalry with Larry was also the first step on **his road to superstardom**. As Jordan would explain in future interviews, he felt his father loved Larry more. While brothers and sisters often feel that way about each other during childhood, this youngster used his feelings of pain and anguish to prove to not only his father, but to the world, why he deserved the love and affection from his father that he felt he wasn't receiving. Jordan often recalls how he used that perception of his father's emotions to drive himself to the limit and excel.

In fact, Larry was a very good athlete as well and playing with him pushed and enhanced Jordan's own abilities in middle and high school. Larry might very well have gone on to being known as the better basketball player if he had only grown just a bit taller. At 5'7", he just didn't have the height to go to an elite level, but even the coaches at Emsley A. Laney High School in Wilmington, where both boys attended, thought that if Larry had surpassed the six foot marker, he, not Michael, would have been the one grabbing all the headlines.

A young Michael Jordan

CHAPTER 2

HIGH SCHOOL YEARS

It has been widely documented how Jordan **failed to make the varsity basketball team** as a sophomore. There have been various explanations for this, such as his height at the time (5'9") was too short or that his skill set was not established, but it was more than likely due to his youth. Only one sophomore made the team at all, and the 6'6" Leroy Smith was certainly the most logical choice. Leroy played basketball with Jordan nearly every day, and they had attended basketball camp together over the summer, but when Jordan experienced a 5-inch growth spurt, and it wasn't from doing chin-ups, after the season, he surpassed his colleague on the varsity team.

Second Source Of Motivation: Not Making Varsity Team As A Sophomore

By his own admission, **the day Jordan didn't make the team is remembered as the very worst day of his life at that point and sparked the competitive drive** he was already known for to an entirely new level. Smith even mentioned that Jordan began to concentrate on every facet of the game with an intensity he had never seen anyone match. Obviously, this was due to Jordan's own personality, his parents instilling him with the value of working very hard, and his mortification of not making the team, especially since both he and Smith thought he was the more talented player.

"We knew Michael was good," Fred Lynch, the Laney assistant coach, said later to David Halberstam for his book *Playing For Keeps, "but we wanted him to play more and we thought the jayvee was better for him."* He easily became the best player on the jayvee that year. He simply dominated the play, and he did it **not by size but with quickness**. There were games in which he would score 40 points. He was so good, in fact, that the jayvee games became quite popular. The entire varsity began to come early so they could watch him play in the jayvee games.

Michael Jordan during his high school days

Jordan Shows What He Is Made Of

Once Jordan made the team, the rest, as they say, is history. According to a 1998 article by Kevin Sherrington of the *Dallas Morning News*, during the first varsity game, Michael scored 35 points, then during his two seasons with the team, he averaged, per game, 25 points, 12 rebounds, and 5.3 assists. Although Jordan certainly had improved from his sophomore to junior year, there were many who he had come through the ranks with, players and coaches alike, who did not feel Jordan would ever develop into the player he became. For example, the shape of his head earned him the nicknames '*Peanut*' or '*Shagnut*,' and the coaching staff never discussed moving him up to varsity, even when he excelled at the junior level, because there were older, more talented players above him. *"Michael judged his game on how he played against the upperclassmen,"* recalled his teammate Michael Bragg. *"He couldn't beat any of them one-on-one until the end of this sophomore year. He was also a* **shy basketball player** *and had trouble beating his brother Larry."*

CHAPTER 3

FIVE-STAR BASKETBALL CAMP

The summer between junior year and senior year, however, Michael Jordan's basketball future did not merely become suspected, but virtually assured, after his invitation to the *Five-Star Basketball Camp* run by *Howard Garfinkel* in Honesdale, Pennsylvania. When Jordan first arrived, he was extremely nervous and **felt he did not belong.** He certainly had many good reasons to be apprehensive about his presence there, as Garfinkel, who was inducted into the National Collegiate College Basketball Hall of Fame in 2014, was a serious mover and shaker in the sport. His camp opened in 1966 and recruited the likes of Chuck Daly – the head coach of the initial Dream Team and an NBA coach for two-time champions the Detroit Pistons, Hubie Brown, and Bobby Knight. Another important feature of Garfinkel's camp was that there was only one other camp, *Bob Cronauer's camp* in Milledgeville, Georgia, that provided national exposure for these aspiring athletes. There was no Amateur Athletic Union back then. The year Jordan attended, 1980, was especially interesting as other members of the roster included Patrick Ewing, Chris Mullin, and Karl Malone.

In later interviews, Jordan referred to that summer in Honesdale as the **"turning point in my life."** He was the first session's MVP, and the only reason he was not given the same distinction in the second session was the result of a rule where players could not collect back-to-back MVP awards. Overall, Jordan won seven awards during his time with Garfinkel. What was of paramount importance, however, was how he was ranked after completing the camp. Garfinkel placed him amongst **the top 10 recruits in the nation,** while two prominent scouts had him ranked in the first position over only Ewing and second behind Ewing.

STEVE JAMES

*Howard Garfinkel at the induction ceremony for
the National Collegiate Basketball Hall of Fame in 2014*

Why Dean Smith Lived In Fear

Garfinkel's camp, which has produced LeBron James, Isiah Thomas, Carmelo Anthony, and Kevin Durant, was definitely an **opportunity Jordan made the most of.** However, the experience was one the recruiting staff at the University of North Carolina were petrified of. Prior to Jordan's invitation to Five-Star, he remained a secret that head coach Dean Smith was loath to reveal to the world. After receiving a tip about Jordan's abilities from Mike Brown, the New Hanover county athletic director, who were Laney's stiffest rivals, assistant coach Bill Guthridge traveled to Laney to watch Jordan play during his junior season. Guthridge revealed to Coach Smith that he was impressed with the **quickness of Jordan's hands and the ease with which he could perform a 360-degree dunk.** That is when Smith, who was very firmly committed to recruiting players from North Carolina, assigned another assistant, Roy Williams, to begin actively pursuing Jordan. Smith also had two other requests of Williams: do not tell anyone in the media about this kid and get him to the North Carolina basketball camp over the upcoming summer.

Williams was successful on both counts. *"Very few people knew about him at that time,"* he told *Inside Carolina* magazine in 2011. *"Michael came and just destroyed everyone at camp."* The staff was also very impressed by Jordan's thirst for knowledge and quest for conquering the fundamentals. Williams, however, was faced with a dilemma when contacted by Herring, Jordan's high school coach, who was seeking advice on Jordan's attendance at Five-Star after procuring an invite for him. Williams recommended the teenager go to Five-Star to test his abilities and to learn the fundamentals of the game. *"So I called Howard Garfinkel and told him Michael was coming and he would be really pleased with him as a player. I told Garf, 'He's going to be good enough to be a waiter.' You see, if you could wait tables, you could go to two weeks for the price of one. So I did call Garf and talked about the opportunity."*

Unfortunately, Williams's boss did not feel the same way about his behavior or suggesting Jordan attend Five-Star. Smith was intent on keeping Jordan's talent under wraps so he would not have to engage in a battle to recruit him. Since UNC was the front runner to sign Jordan, Smith was fearful that other schools would pounce on the youngster and sway his decision. He realized Jordan would not remain a secret forever and wanted to tighten his grip on him before competing with the rest of the world. *"Coach, in my opinion, he was going to go and I was just trying to give him some guidance about what I thought would be best for him,"* Williams said. *"And Michael's family really appreciated it."*

Smith, who was known for his sagacity both on and off the sidelines, saw **his**

worst fears come to fruition when Jordan's skills were witnessed by the basketball world. According to *Inside Carolina* magazine, the Hall of Fame coach suddenly experienced intense competition from South Carolina, where Bill Foster, who had previously commanded the sidelines at Duke University, introduced the teen to the governor and from Jim Valvano at N.C. State, who had a solid plan for Jordan to emulate the well-esteemed David Thompson. The University of Maryland also threw their hat into the ring when Jordan's father was approached by Lefty Driesell that, when the Chesapeake Bay Bridge opened, the campus would be the same distance from his hometown as Chapel Hill.

Despite the ulcers Coach Smith staved off during Jordan's recruiting period, ultimately, **Michael selected North Carolina** and probably never seriously considered any other institution. Jordan was very excited to become a Tar Heel, but his family's influence also played a major role in his decision. They were pleased with the school and, unlike Smith initially thought, with how Williams had responded to Herring's request. *"Michael's dad was always very appreciative,"* Williams said. In fact, James Jordan was so appreciative that the elder Jordan handcrafted a wood-burning stove for Williams's home and continued to construct a new appliance for every house Williams lived in thereafter.

Williams, Folger, Guthridge and Smith were the men responsible for Jordan attending the University of North Carolina.

Senior Year And Still
Not Grabbing The Headlines

As Jordan sailed through his senior year at Laney, while being courted by major universities such as Duke, Syracuse, and Virginia, he dazzled spectators, players, and scouts alike with his conversation-starting dunks, dexterity, and scoring ability. However, just as Jordan was not the top-ranked prospect in terms of recruiting, Jordan did not receive top billing on the day he signed his scholarship with North Carolina in 1981 or for his 30-point record performance in the McDonald's All-American game. His final free throws eventually helped tie the game, and later, to win the game outright, and he also contributed 6 steals and 4 assists, but in the end, the MVP award went to Adrian Branch and Aubrey Sherrod. He also finished second behind Buzz Peterson, who would later become his close friend and roommate, as the Associated Press's state prep player of the season. By the time he graduated from Laney, however, Jordan had grown to a healthy 6'6", which was much taller than anyone had been in the Jordan family, and his high school coach loftily predicted North Carolina would win the national championship in 1982. Jordan would not disappoint his former instructor; he later scored the game winning shot over Patrick Ewing as a freshman to bring home the title to Chapel Hill.

*Michael Jordan presenting his McDonald's All-America jersey
to the Naismith Basketball Hall of Fame executive director in 1985*

UNIVERSITY OF NORTH CAROLINA

at

CHAPEL HILL, N. C.   27514

Basketball Office
(919) 933-1154

Dean E. Smith
Head Basketball Coach

Assistants:
Bill Guthridge
Eddie Fogler

August 12, 1980

Mr. Michael Jordan
4647 Gordon Road
Wilmington, NC 28405

Dear Michael:

Our staff surely enjoyed visiting with you and your family there at your beautiful home. It was a delightful evening and one which we were able to use to get to know you better. Hopefully you felt more comfortable with us also and that you will seriously consider the University of North Carolina for your college education.

If there are any questions which came up following our departure, please give me a collect call and I will be happy to discuss them with you. Otherwise we may give you a follow-up call before too long just to touch base.

We do think you are a tremendous young man and are impressed not only with your obvious basketball talent but the way you have been a leader at school and done well academically. We look forward to following you closely this year and hope to see you frequently in Chapel Hill.

I am writing your parents separately since they were so very hospitable to us. Enjoyed seeing you, Michael, and hope that beginning in September 1981 I can be your coach.

Most sincerely,

Dean E. Smith

DES/kl

Michael —
Have written A & T
for Larry —
DS

A copy of Dean Smith's recruitment letter to Michael Jordan after a campus visit.

14

Michael Jordan and Dean Smith.

CHAPTER 4

CHAPEL HILL

Although Jordan certainly had an exceptional career at North Carolina, it was rather anti-climactic after March 29, 1982, when Carolina won the NCAA championship. Jordan was proclaimed the ***ACC Freshman of the Year*** despite upperclassmen James Worthy and Sam Perkins taking a much larger leadership role and deservedly so, as they were All-Americans. Throughout his freshman campaign, Jordan averaged 13.4 points from a 53.4% shooting percentage and naturally played a role in the Tar Heels advancing to the championship game. His team would meet the Georgetown Hoyas, whose freshman center Patrick Ewing, attended the Five-Star Basketball Camp with Jordan back in the summer of 1980. With sixteen seconds left in the game, Jordan, who was battling a throat infection, coolly connected on an 18-foot jump shot to take the lead and ultimately produce a victory over the Hoyas after Worthy intercepted Fred Brown's errant pass on Georgetown's final drive. **The shot brought him instant recognition** around the world and was merely a hint of the magic that Jordan would later bring to basketball.

Michael Jordan shooting a jumper in the 1982 National Championship game.

Michael Jordan going up for a dunk - his freshman season at North Carolina.

Michael Jordan taking the game winning shot against
Georgetown in the 1982 National Championship Game.

After "The Shot"

Jordan remained at Chapel Hill for two more seasons. He was named *College Player of the Year* by the *Sporting News* as a sophomore, but his team failed to return to the finals. As a junior, Jordan collected a second consecutive *College Player of the Year* award, the *Wooden Award*, and the *Naismith Award*, but, again, North Carolina did not advance to the championship game. After feeling there was nothing more to accomplish at the collegiate level, he decided to end his amateur career and head to the NBA to play professional basketball. His mother was deeply opposed to this decision as she was steadfastly determined he obtain his degree, but his father and even Dean Smith supported Jordan's decision; **there was simply nothing left for him to accomplish at the collegiate level.**

CHAPTER 5

NBA CAREER

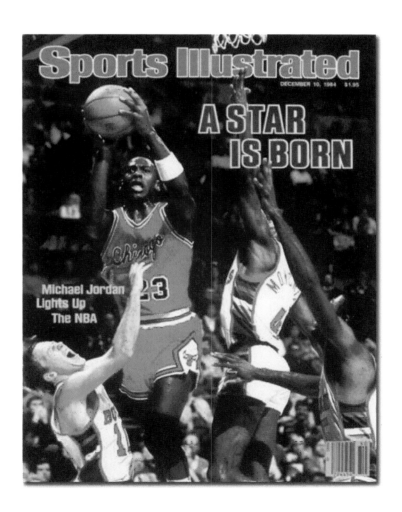

Many are astonished when they learn that **Jordan was *not* the first pick during the NBA Draft of 1984**. The Houston Rockets chose Hakeem Olajuwon from the University of Houston, who is a Hall of Fame player, and the Portland Trailblazers chose Sam Bowie from the University of Kentucky. Unfortunately, the very talented Bowie never was able to live up to his potential due to frequent knee injuries. Jordan was the third selection in the draft and headed to Chicago to suit up for the Bulls. When Jordan stepped off the plane at O'Hare Airport, to commence **one of the most spectacular careers in the history of all athletics**, he suddenly realized that the Bulls had sent no envoy to greet him. A young limo driver noticed Jordan and how nervous he seemed. George Koehler had no idea how much his life would change that day as he approached Jordan and offered him a ride. Koehler drove him to his new home on Essex Drive that evening, and the two have been the best of friends ever since.

It did not take long for the fans, the Bulls organization, the league, and the rest of the planet to notice Michael Jordan. In fact, even early on in the season, Jordan managed to score 27 points in a loss to the Celtics in Chicago, but could not have made more of an impression than he did in defeat. *"I've never seen one player turn a team around like that,"* Larry Bird said after the game. *"All the Bulls have become better because of him. Pretty soon this place will be packed every night. They'll pay just to watch Jordan. Heck, there was one drive tonight. He had the ball up in his right hand, then he took it down. Then he brought it back up. I got a hand on it, fouled him, and he still scored. All the while, he's in the air. You have to play this game to know how difficult that is. You see that and say, 'Well, what the heck can you do?'"*

The Death Of His Father
And Career Changes

On July 23, 1993, an unthinkable tragedy occurred. James R. Jordan, Michael's father, was brutally murdered and dumped into a swamp in a robbery. As previously stated, Michael Jordan was very close with his father, and the news of his death rocked him to his core. Shaken, and in a state of unimaginable grief, Michael Jordan shocked the world by announcing **his retirement from basketball**, and shortly thereafter, **began playing baseball**. This career change was, more than likely, a way for a grieving Michael to fulfill his father's dream that he become a baseball player, as his father was a much bigger fan of baseball than basketball. However, Michael Jordan, as he had focused his attention on basketball for so long, was no longer the baseball superstar he had been in his youth. In addition, Jordan had picked up a worrisome habit during his time in the NBA – gambling. He failed to make the big leagues and wasn't exactly fantastic in the minor leagues either. His life was confusing and tumultuous, and, for the first time, Jordan's life wasn't working out the way he thought it would be. Jordan claimed he would never return to basketball, yet his failures in baseball seemed to suggest that Michael Jordan would turn back on his original promise to never return to the NBA.

However, when **Jordan returned to the Chicago Bulls,** he proved that not only was he able to navigate through an experience that took its toll on him emotionally and mentally, he proved that he could come back stronger and better than ever. By realizing where his priorities lay, as well as understanding that, sometimes, you must take time off to recharge and try something new, His Airness was able to navigate the difficulty of loss.

Career Highlights

While it may seem unnecessary to rehash the specifics of Jordan's **fifteen-year NBA career**, his multiple retirements, his stint playing professional baseball after his father's death, and his ascension to ownership and management in the NBA, as most people are aware of Michael Jordan's amazing legacy, it still is worthwhile to mention his successes. For more than a decade, Jordan was **not only the most famous athlete on the globe, but one of the most famous people**. In a career where he was Rookie of the Year, while third in points scored behind only Bernard King and Larry Bird, Jordan was also a member of the 1984 Gold Medal Olympic team, known as the Dream Team. He was a five-time league MVP (Most Valuable Player) and was the finals MVP for all six of his championships, the Defensive Player of the League on one occasion, and was on the All-Defensive Team nine times. Jordan collected ten scoring titles, possessed the most steals on three occasions, and was a fourteen-time All-Star.

CHAPTER 6

UNLOCKING THE MYSTIQUE OF HIS AIRNESS

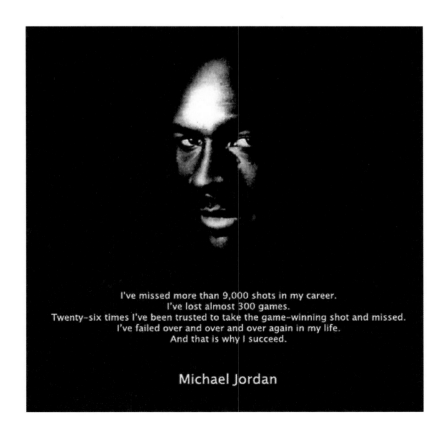

I've missed more than 9,000 shots in my career.
I've lost almost 300 games.
Twenty-six times I've been trusted to take the game-winning shot and missed.
I've failed over and over and over again in my life.
And that is why I succeed.

Michael Jordan

Michael's Basketball Philosophy

Michael Jordan's personal philosophies when it comes to his basketball game are philosophies that are not only applicable to basketball, but are also applicable to anyone trying to accomplish a goal in any setting. Jordan's ideas are simple – **work tirelessly and prove everyone who doesn't believe in you wrong**. One could talk for hours about the specific defensive or offensive techniques that Michael Jordan uses in his game, but just like any other person, Michael Jordan's game evolved as he himself evolved. However, the aforementioned ideas are two things that have remained the same in his philosophy towards basketball, and this has allowed Jordan to reach heights that no other person in the history of basketball had ever been able to do.

Michael Jordan's **biggest accomplishments in his career are arguably the things he accomplished that no one believed he could**. When the people at his high school argued that he could not make the varsity basketball team – he proved them wrong. When he was criticized for being weak defensively in the NBA, he won defensive player of the year. The idea is simple: **take criticism as a chance to improve, and don't let it get you down**. Criticism isn't proof that you cannot achieve something – it's just proof that you still have something to work on.

Even more important than using criticism as a motivating factor, however, is **being motivated to work constantly**. Rome was not built in a day, and Michael Jordan wasn't born as *"Air Jordan."* No, when Michael Jordan was born, he was simply the fourth child out of five who grew up on the North Carolina coast. However, by working harder than everyone else around him, and by taking advantage of every opportunity to grow that he came across, the name "Michael Jordan" is now a name that has special meaning in the minds of people worldwide. Consider this – Michael has held the top spot of most popular boy's name more frequently than any other name in the past 100 years in the United States, and the surname Jordan is also one of the most common last names for citizens of the United States. Yet, Michael Jordan, through his hard work and ability to work through tough times, was able to "make a name for himself" and forever transform the perception of his "common" name. **Becoming extraordinary can be achieved by working hard and being dedicated to what you love, and that's the only way to get there.**

Basketball Techniques

Michael Jordan's basketball technique was simple; become good at the basics so that you can jazz up your technique with something fancy. Key sports analysts have outlined **the basic principles to Michael Jordan's techniques,** and they can be summed up as follows:

- Three spot finishing
- The wing spinout
- "Off the Dribble" attack

These scoring techniques all combined *flawless footwork with amazing fakes,* and *ridiculously precise shots* – all in the same play. After taking these three core techniques, then adding *spins,* and *the classic 40+ inch vertical jump* that His Airness was known for, Michael Jordan's on-the-court techniques were sealed.

His Workouts

Michael Jordan was known for waking up at the crack of dawn (or even earlier) to begin working out at 5:30 a.m. in order to commence a vigorous and intense workout. He began with doing dumbbell step-ups, split jumps, and lying glute stretches, and then would continue with an intense, muscle-building workout that included squats and squat jumps. Each of these exercises were done three times each, with fifteen reps per cycle. This was how Michael Jordan warmed up before even setting foot on the basketball court.

Michael Jordan's Fears
And Superstitions

Michael Jordan's fears are few and far between, but he, like any other human being, does have them. His **biggest fear is simple: <u>water</u>**, specifically swimming. When Michael Jordan was young, he, sadly, watched a friend drown in a lake, while nearly drowning himself. Ever since then, he has been terrified of large bodies of water and the thought of drowning.

Michael also was no stranger to superstition and lucky rituals; he wore his **University of North Carolina shorts beneath his uniform during each game he played in**. Michael Jordan started the trend of long basketball shorts, but most do not know that the reason behind them was simply to cover up His Airness's good luck charm.

LIFE AFTER BASKETBALL

In January of 2015, Michael Jordan fought back tears as he stood behind a podium in Charlotte, South Carolina. Known simply to many as the greatest basketball player to have ever lived, the Wilmington, North Carolina, native has amassed a plethora of awards throughout his storied career. He claimed this one, however, held the most emotional appeal, as he was being honored as the city's Businessperson of the Year for his ownership of the Charlotte Hornets. *"For all of the people that think that I'm in this for the short term, you better pull your socks up and just hang around — because my promise to this organization and this community is to bring a winner,"* Jordan said.

Nike And The Birth Of
The Air Jordan Brand

...g before Michael Jordan purchased the Hornets, then known as the Charlotte Bobcats, in 2010, he established his **business career with Nike**. After returning from the Olympics, Jordan met with Converse and rejected their offer for a shoe deal as their percentage of the market was declining due to their reluctance to use leather. Jordan entered into negotiations with Adidas, whose shoe he preferred because it was built low to the ground, but after the intercession of O.J. Simpson, Jordan was pinpointed as the must-have athlete to sign to a lucrative shoe deal. Whatever Simpson's legacy may be, the facts are that he was paid to wear Sports-Bilt shoes throughout his career and received a check from them annually, as his endorsement of the products made the company quite a bit of money. They also had a relationship with Nike, who was the new kid on the block in the sneaker business, and Nike witnessed Sports-Bilt's pursuit of Jordan, and Nike made the executive decision to make the young man an offer that was hard to refuse.

The Contract Of A Lifetime

Throughout Jordan's contract with Nike, he was paid ***$500,000 per year in cash***, which was unheard of that time. James Worthy's deal with New Balance, for example, was the most lucrative of that era, and was only $180,000 for eight years. The company included stock options and other perks to bring Jordan's total sum to a potential $7 million over five years, provided certain conditions were met. The first was that Nike could simply decide to terminate the contract two years early if Jordan did not meet one of these three goals: **average 20 points per game for an entire year, become an NBA All-Star, or be named Rookie of the Year**. Jordan went back to Adidas and asked if they could be competitive with this deal. Since they could not, he took the offer from Nike.

Jordan appreciated the tremendous amount of input the company allowed him to have during the creation of the red-and-black Air Jordan. When they debuted for $65 a pair in March of 1985, no sneaker had ever had that high a price tag. By May, however, Nike had netted more than $70 million from their new product, even after battling with the NBA after the league banned the shoes because the color scheme was not to their liking. By the end of 1985, Nike had cleared $100 million. According to ESPN.com, the company states that the business relationship between Nike and Jordan was *"the perfect combination of quality product, marketing and athlete endorsement."*

ESPN.com noted, *"In 2012, the Jordan brand sold $2.5 billion worth of shoes at retail, its best year ever, according to market retail tracking firm SportsOneSource. Air Jordans made up 58 percent of all basketball shoes bought in the U.S. and 77 percent of all kids' basketball shoes. Most of those kids didn't even see Michael Jordan play. 'Sonny kept saying, 'He's the guy, he's the guy,' White said. 'But we didn't know what that really meant. None of us thought it would be like it has been.'"* Jordan never did either and always had strongly preferred Adidas prior to signing his deal with Nike. The contract with Nike and its slogan "Be Like Mike" are one of the primary reasons **Jordan officially reached billionaire status in 2015** and was **added to the Forbes list of wealthiest people in the world in 2014**. Interestingly enough, it was O.J. Simpson who originally predicted that Jordan would break the record books both in sports and business. Who would have imagined that?

Air Jordan: One of the Top 10 Most Expensive Basketball Shoes Ever Made.

In Basketball Front Offices

Although Jordan has been criticized for his management techniques when he was with the Washington Wizards, especially by drafting Kwame Brown with the top selection, he has always managed to subvert any negative assessments of himself. His purchase of the Washington Wizards is another example of his business acumen, as when Jordan purchased the team, the worth of NBA franchises was at a near all-time low. Jordan purchased the team for $275 million in 2010 and saw its worth grow to $410 million by 2014. After the Los Angeles Clippers were sold to Steve Balmer for $2 billion this year, the Hornets value increased to $725 million. According to *Business Insider, "That is looking like a wise investment, especially considering the league's massive new TV deal with ESPN and Turner. In the deal, which begins in 2016, the networks will pay the NBA an average of $2.66 billion per year. They paid about $930 million per year under the old deal. That works out to an extra $57 million in revenue per year for MJ's Hornets."*

CHAPTER 8

WHAT MAKES MJ
SO SPECIAL

"You have competition every day because you set such high standards for yourself that you have to go every day and live up to that"

– Michael Jordan

Five weeks before his 50th birthday, on February 17, 2013, Wright Thompson sat down with Michael Jordan to perform an in-depth interview for ESPN's *Outside the Lines*. No one knows what Thompson anticipated or what his level of familiarity with Jordan exactly was, but he does reveal an undisclosed assumption His Airness had concluded long before his professional basketball career commenced. *"I...I always thought I would die young,"* he told Wright, who then chronicled how irate his mother would get when he would explain to her he just could not imagine ever suffering from the physical aspects of aging. *"He seemed too powerful, too young, and death was more likely than a slow decline,"* Wright wrote. *"The universe might take him, but it would not permit him to suffer the graceless loss and failure of aging. A tragic flaw could undo him but never anything as common as bad knees or failing eyesight."*

Wright is simply describing how **Jordan is harnessing the competitive fire**, or raging inferno, that has been contained within him since he felt his father loved his older brother more and was left off the varsity team. This need to be the best, to always win and always prove he was superior, is certainly one of the primary secrets to Jordan's unquestionable success. It has never been denied that his behavior has sometimes been so aggressive in the heat of the moment it could be characterized as mean, but this competitiveness, which flirts with the limits of mental obsession, is at the core of Jordan's being.

Rather than allow it to be his undoing, His Airness snatched that rage, embraced it, and transformed it into something productive, useful, and rewarding. Wright's article describes how that spirit remains clearly visible, but that Jordan is attempting to change. Remember, however, this man was on a mission to weigh 218, which was his playing weight by this 50th birthday, and always stated he could play basketball at age 50 or beyond. Nothing can ever be ruled out with Jordan, because he will not allow rules or boundaries to fence him in.

What Sets Him Apart

For Jordan being competitive is primal – a component of his nature he cannot control, only manage. There are numerous tales of how competitive Michael Jordan was and still is. For example, during a training camp scrimmage, Steve Kerr had some choice words for Jordan, and rather than respond with his own pointed rejoinder, Jordan punched Kerr in the face. Kerr, however, was thankful to Jordan for forcing him to stand up and take responsibility for his behavior. According to *The Dan Patrick Show*, he said, *"It was the best thing that could have happened to me."* At a 2011 charity golf event, Jordan bet a fan $500 cash he could hit it on the green, and, of course, he did. According to Rick Reilly of ESPN, he destroyed Rodney McCray's professional career because, during $100 practice shoot-around games, he would scream in his face, taunting him, how big of a loser he was, and McCray could not physically perform after taking the verbal abuse. Muggsy Bogues claims Jordan ruined his shot permanently after pushing him to shoot and calling him a midget. Then, of course, there is the 1997 Finals where Jordan was ill with the flu, but, like in college, when he had a throat infection in the National Championship game, he shrugged it off and scored 38 to lead the Bulls to victory. Just several days later, they captured the series.

Difficulty To Control
His Competiveness

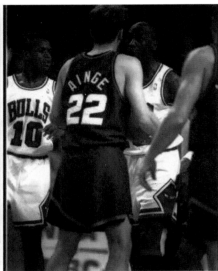

The descriptions of Jordan's **natural propensity to dominate in every facet of his life** are well documented and plentiful. It even affected his personal relationships. Wright's article discusses how Jordan initially never would have allowed a woman he was in a relationship with to win an argument, but that with his second wife Yvette he does allow her to talk him into things. He claims that is "progress" for him. Wright also explains how Jordan stated, *"I can't help myself. It's like an addiction. You ask for this special power to achieve these heights and now you got it and you want to give it back, but you can't. If I could then I could breathe. How can I find peace without the game of basketball?"*

So, for Michael Jordan, the greatest player ever to participate in the sport, an endorsement icon and a billionaire, the very demon that plagues him internally is the very reason for his stupendous success. Many people would consider that a conundrum and it is, but Jordan is so mentally strong that **he turned his biggest weakness into a blessing**. He chose the direction his life would take when he did not make the basketball team in high school. When he spoke with his mother about what had happened, she told him to go out and prove they were wrong for not selecting him, rather than sit and sulk about it. The idea of **never giving up**, even facing discouragement, is the simple rule Michael Jordan has lived by his whole life and is what propelled him to heights not many individuals on this earth could hope to attain.

Although Jordan's basketball playing days appear to be over, Michael Jordan continues to shock and surprise the world with his amazing skills. He recently beat a Bobcat player in a one-on-one match shortly before his 50th birthday. Unfortunately, the harsh realities of aging set in when he was so sore the next day he needed treatment from a trainer to relieve the pain he felt. The passing of time, however, is unable to touch the legacy that Jordan has created for himself. Jordan might not be the nicest person at times, and can be gruff and fly into rages, but his work ethic is undeniable and the allure of the type of success he enjoys is impossible to refute. He has captivated the entire planet with his professional exploits, persona, and behavior. In fact, Jordan is undoubtedly a role model for hundreds of thousands, if not millions, of people, who hope to merely obtain a fraction of the type of success he has enjoyed. They don't just look up to him or are envious of his accomplishments; they have internalized the aura of Michael Jordan and have convinced themselves if Michael Jordan could do it, then so can I.

Jordan's Basketball Legacy

While **Kobe Bryant and LeBron James are often compared to Michael Jordan** and endless heated discussions wage over if Jordan really was the best basketball player ever, there is simply no comparison. Both these men are extremely gifted athletes and have accomplished things mere mortals can only fantasize about, but neither one can compare to "His Airness" or "Air Jordan." It was not only what Jordan accomplished on the court, with his incredible consistency, drive, passion, and devotion to the game, but it is also what he brought to the game and the aura he carried about him that garnered him accolades as the greatest athlete of the century, and possibly best of all time, by every reputable sports media organization in the world. Jordan's incredible dunks, his habit of hanging his tongue out of his mouth, and the fact that he won game after game set the stage for the modern evolution of the NBA into the business it is today. Arguably, without Michael Jordan, Bryant and James would not have been able to become the extremely talented NBA players they are today. Jordan has also been cited as an inspiration for athletes in other sports, including Cam Newton of the Carolina Panthers, an NFL team, and Michael Phelps, the swimming Olympic gold medalist.

There is also another thing that sets Jordan on a pedestal over his notable peers and that is his penchant for business. Jordan, through being a spokesman for Nike and various other products, has marketed himself to the tune of more than a billion dollars of net worth. He is valued and respected in the business community as a role model for all entrepreneurs. Jordan did not merely excel at basketball, but he was also outstanding at making the most out of an opportunity and dominating the competition. There is no one like Michael Jeffrey Jordan, and he is the reason Bryant, LeBron, and other successful basketball players have the endorsements they do today.

Top 10 Motivational Lessons

Jordan possesses an **intense amount of power as a motivational figure for people outside of the sports world.** For instance, a cursory internet search reveals several pages of ways Michael Jordan can be incorporated into anyone's mentality to lift them to new heights. People want to learn from him. They crave what he so valiantly portrays and that is why he is quoted frequently, seriously, and intently. People still want to be like Mike more than two decades after the slogan first was introduced to the world.

Here are **some of the most popular motivational quotes from Michael Jordan** and the lessons that can be extracted from them:

– Have Faith in Life, Work, or Sports:

"Be true to the game, because the game will be true to you. If you try to shortcut the game, the game will shortcut you. If you put forth the effort, good things will be bestowed upon you. If you do the work, you get rewarded. There are no shortcuts in life."

– Take Failure as a Positive Rather than a Negative:

"I've missed more than 9,000 shots in my career. I have lost 300 games. On 26 occasions I have been entrusted to take the game-winning shot…and missed. And I have failed over and over and over again in my life. And that is why I succeed. Failure only makes me work harder."

— There Is No Such Thing as Fear:

"I know fear is an obstacle for some people, but to me it is an illusion."

— Do Not Let Anything Hold You Back:

"Some people want it to happen, some people wish it would happen and some people make it happen."

— You Must Have Confidence in Yourself to Achieve Your Dreams:

"You have to expect things of yourself before you can do them."

— Never Refuse Help From Others:

"If you think and achieve as a team, the individual accolades will take care of themselves. Talent wins games, but teamwork and intelligence wins championships."

— Master the Basics Before Moving Forward:

"You can practice shooting eight hours a day, but if your technique is wrong, then all you become is very good at shooting the wrong way. Get the fundamentals down and the level of everything you do will rise."

— There is No Such Phrase as Can't:

"Obstacles don't have to stop you. If you run into a wall, don't turn around and give up. Figure out how to climb it, go through it, or work around it."

— Don't Ever Shy Away from Hard Work:

"Champions do not become champions when they win an event, but in the hours, weeks, and months, and years they spend preparing for it. The victorious performance itself is merely a demonstration of their championship character."

— Recognize Your Weaknesses and Make Positive Changes:

"My attitude is that if you push me towards something that you think is a weakness, then I will turn that perceived weakness into a strength."

CHAPTER 9

SECRETS TO DEVELOPING A MINDSET LIKE MICHAEL'S

It cannot be refuted that Jordan's **competitive nature fueled his rise to elite levels** in the sport of basketball and in the business world, but he also acknowledges that passion is sometimes exceptionally difficult for him to control. This is where the major factor contributing to his success enters the picture and that is his mind-set. Jordan was a **highly focused, rigid individual who set his mind on his goals and would not allow anyone or anything to dissuade him.** He also knew when to **manage his nature or at least harness his emotions.** Without a crucial component such as the correct mind-set, Jordan would just have been another talented athlete who never achieved his full potential or would have been satisfied with what he did achieve.

According to the research performed by Carol S. Dweck, a professor of psychology at Stanford University, *"there are two types of mindsets people can have about their talents and abilities. Those with a fixed mindset believe that their talents and abilities are simply fixed. They have a certain amount and that's that. People with a growth mindset, on the other hand, think of talents and abilities as things they can develop – as potentials that come to fruition through effort, practice, and instruction."* Dweck then goes on to explain that all the great athletes, such as Tiger Woods, Michael Jordan, and Mia Hamm, possess a growth mind-set. This means they don't simply rely on their talent and are **constantly trying to challenge themselves so they can learn how to improve.**

For instance, if a person with a fixed mind-set is faced with the choice between a task that will make them appear smarter or a challenging task that will teach them something, they will select the opportunity that allows them to appear smarter. They do not have the mind-set to see this as an educational experience they can benefit from down the road, but feel their levels of intelligence are already what they are and cannot be improved. Therefore, they do not have the willingness to learn more and do not feel pushed to take a challenge where they could very well fail because they are not up to it. A person with a growth mind-set, however, would select the challenging task. This type of mind-set is characteristic of individuals that thirst for knowledge, they want their boundaries to constantly be tested and to be introduced to new things. They always want to be better. They can **never accept that what they possess is all they are capable of having**.

Dweck says, *"Our studies show that it is precisely because of their focus on learning that growth mindset students end up with higher performance. They take charge of the learning process. For example, they study more deeply, manage their time better, and keep up their motivation. If they do poorly at first, they find out why and fix it. In a study of students entering an elite university, we found that students with a fixed mindset preferred to hide their deficiencies, rather than take an opportunity to remedy them — even when the deficiency put their future success at risk."*

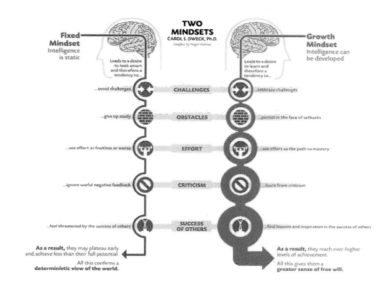

How To Be Like Mike

It may seem as if a mind-set similar to, if not the same as, Michael Jordan's is an impossible mission, but Dweck claims that notion couldn't be further from the truth. *"New work in psychology and neuroscience is demonstrating the tremendous plasticity of the brain – its capacity to change and even reorganize itself when people put serious labor into developing a set of skills."* Other groundbreaking work (for example, by Anders Ericsson) is showing that in virtually every field – sports, science, or the arts – only one thing seems to distinguish the people we later call geniuses from their other talented peers. **This one thing is called practice.** Are mind-sets fixed or can they be changed? *"Mindsets can be fairly stable, but they are beliefs, and beliefs can be changed."*

So, how can an individual or group alter their mind-set if theirs is by nature fixed rather than one of growth? Admittedly, the process is not as simple as it may appear as belief systems that are inculcated over an extended time can be very difficult to subvert or entirely eradicate. It takes time and effort. It just depends on how much the reward is worth. **The correct mind-set is so powerful** it can completely obliterate any negative thoughts or obstacles, so here are some *steps to incorporate to reach that goal*:

- Decide Exactly What You Want and Never Lose Sight of It:

The majority of people are unhappy with their job, their pay, their relationship status, or how they look. They often have no true direction and are often doing something because it seems like that is what they are supposed to be doing. These people are only existing, not living, and many of them probably have no idea what would really make them happy. In order to obtain **a growth mind-set**, a person must figure out what they want and then what they must do to get it. It may not be easy and failure may accompany that effort, but if an attempt is never made, one will never know. Don't allow fear to limit what will bring happiness. **No mountain is too high, and no goal is unrealistic. Set that standard and then go about making it occur.**

- **Do Not Let the Negative Impact You:**

In order to transition to a growth mind-set, **all negativity must be banished**. When faced with a challenge or crisis, do not allow that to become overwhelming or feel defeated. Even if the odds appear insurmountable, always take the positive approach, **stay relaxed, and be calm**. That, again, may sound easier said than done, but if the process is taken one day at a time and one's thought process is continually examined, then, getting back on track after a setback will become second nature. It will be automatic. If a negative thought should worm its way through, do not stress about it. Simply acknowledge it, let it go, and move forward. There is no time for negativity if success is to occur.

- **In Order to Be the Best, You Need Support:**

It is impossible to be positive all the time when people are always complaining and not willing to work or look on the bright side of things. **A person must surround themselves with positivity.** They must do this not only for their own benefit, but also to build the growth mind-set in the environment around them. Positive people make others want to be around them. They are a source of comfort and confidence. There may be some relatives who cannot be neutralized in this situation. They are the only ones that can control their behavior. Each person is an individual, and they have the power to judge whether they will be impacted or not. Simply do not allow people that are not positive to infiltrate the brain or stir up emotions that can impede progress.

In Jordan's case, **his mind-set was developed by his family, teachers, and coaches.** They supported him in his goals, praised him when he did well, and provided every opportunity they could to build his self-confidence. They did not want him to rely on his basic intelligence and abilities, but rather to strive to supersede those limitations. Jordan also possessed a **tremendous amount of determination and willpower.** He wanted to dominate, but he just needed to know how he could do that. Hence, his strong work ethic and the many extra hours he put in the gym and weight room. Also, when he received opportunities, such as the Five-Star Camp, he did not pass them by. His Airness is the classic example of what determination and the correct mind-set can accomplish for anyone. Everyone may not be striving for success on the basketball court, but Michael Jordan's tactics for success apply to the business world, to life, to relationships, and even to education. You may never be able to be Michael Jordan, but you certainly possess the means to achieve your own success through a path modeled after his approach. **All it takes is time, energy, and motivation for you to be like Mike!**

CONCLUSION

Michael Jordan and his incredible basketball career prove that not only is Michael Jordan an inspirational figure to look up to, but that you too can use the techniques he used in your own life to be successful. Understanding the importance of practice and hard work, how to navigate failure, and how to maintain the correct attitude towards your current situation will help you become "like Mike." We hope that this book has not only provided you with important insight into the world's greatest basketball player, but also with insight for your own life.

ABOUT THE AUTHOR

Steve James isn't your typical sports fan. While there are some that will always make time to watch the big game, James started following the NBA at a very young age and has watched some of the best players in the history of the NBA from the very beginning. Even at that young age, he started paying attention to who was really standing out on the court – greats like Michael Jordan, Magic Johnson, or Larry Bird. Steve follows the game to this day and knows the ins and outs of the greatest NBA stars of today, like Kobe Bryant, LeBron James, Kevin Durant, or Stephen Curry. Having carefully watched these players on the court and studied their lives, he has a unique perspective into their success, how it was achieved, and what makes them so great.

He has an insider view into the secrets that have made these players so successful. By collecting this information in his books, he hopes to help not just young, aspiring basketball players, but all people to learn the secrets of what it takes to be successful. By looking at how these players have reached their goals, the readers will glean the information they need to reach their own goals. Steve's years of analyzing play styles, successes, failures, training routines, etc. gives him a real insight into these players!

Printed in Great Britain
by Amazon

72623363R00037